I0467311

Design & Concepts L.L.C
July Issue 2014

House of
Lisabeth Design
Magazine

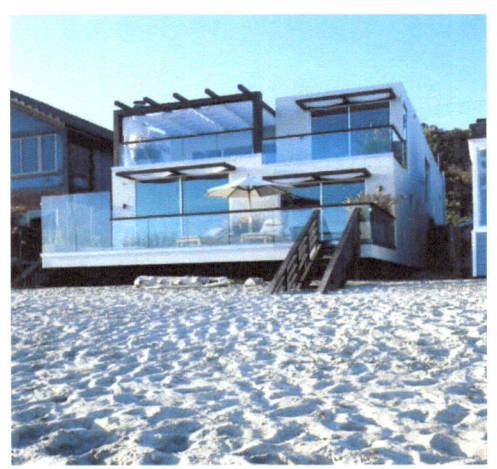

Today's Issue:

- *Doggy's world*
- *Fashion No's*
- *Design or Not*
- *Featured Business*

House of Lisabeth Design Magazine 2014

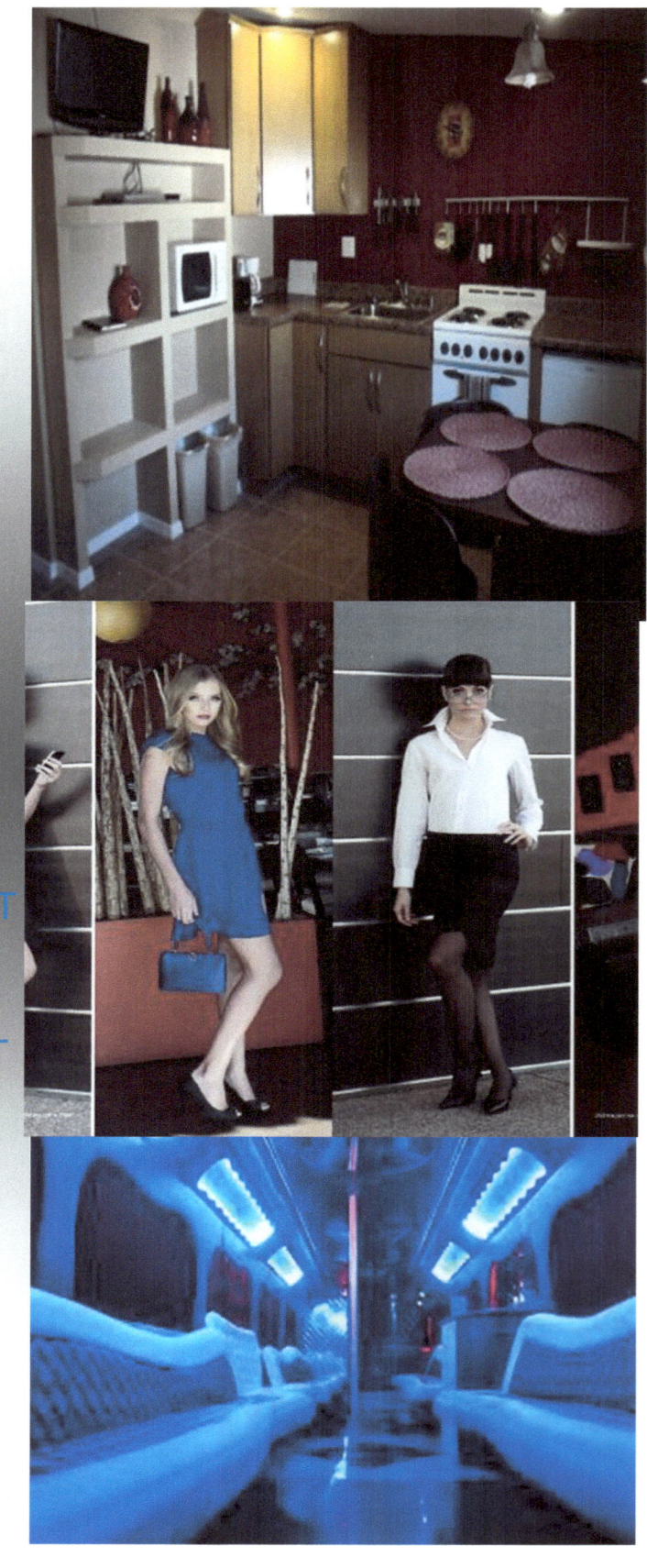

Health Trends: What We Know And What You Need To Know

Nails, and the fungus that hides underneath

Nail fungus is a fungal infection in one or more of your nails. An infection with nail fungus may begin as a white or yellow spot under the tip of your fingernail or toenail. As the nail fungus spreads deeper into your nail, it may cause your nail to discolor, thicken and develop crumbling edges — an unsightly and potentially painful problem.

An infection with nail fungus may be difficult to treat, and it may recur. But medications are available to help clear up nail fungus.

Symptoms

There are different classifications of nail fungus — depending on type of fungus and manifestation — which may have somewhat different signs and symptoms. In general, however, you may have a nail fungal infection — also called onychomycosis (on-i-ko-mi-KO-sis) — if one or more of your nails are:

Thickened

Brittle, crumbly or ragged

Distorted in shape

Dull, with no luster or shine

A dark color, caused by debris building up under your nail

Infected nails also may separate from the nail bed, a condition called onycholysis. You may feel pain in your toes or fingertips and detect a slightly foul odor.

When to see a doctor

Once a nail fungal infection begins, it can persist indefinitely if not treated. See your doctor at the first sign of nail fungus, which is often a tiny white or yellow spot under the tip of your nail.

Health Trends: What We Know And What You Need To Know

Carpel Tunnel Syndrome, what we can do about it

Carpal tunnel syndrome occurs when the median nerve, which runs from the forearm into the palm of the hand, becomes pressed or squeezed at the wrist. The median nerve controls sensations to the palm side of the thumb and fingers (although not the little finger), as well as impulses to some small muscles in the hand that allow the fingers and thumb to move. The carpal tunnel - a narrow, rigid passageway of ligament and bones at the base of the hand - houses the median nerve and tendons.

Carpal tunnel syndrome is often the result of a combination of factors that increase pressure on the median nerve and tendons in the carpal tunnel, rather than a problem with the nerve itself. Most likely the disorder is due to a congenital predisposition - the carpal tunnel is simply smaller in some people than in others. Other contributing factors include trauma or injury to the wrist that cause swelling, such as sprain or fracture; over activity of the pituitary gland; hypothyroidism; rheumatoid arthritis; mechanical problems in the wrist joint; work stress; repeated use of vibrating hand tools; fluid retention during pregnancy or menopause; or the development of a cyst or tumor in the canal. In some cases no cause can be identified.

How to treat Carpel Tunnel Syndrome
There are two ways of treating there is the surgical and non-surgical way. Either way treatment should began as soon as possible also avoiding activities that worsen condition.

To prevent Carpel Tunnel Syndrome remember to take frequent breaks while on job, stretch and wear splints to keep wrist straight. Also remember to use correct posture and keep wrist straight.

Our Pick of this summers 12 hottest men to keep us cool!

This year we wanted to bring together some men that we thought would keep us cool this summer. We narrowed our choices down to 12 men who are hot, successful and definitely going to make this summer sizzle!

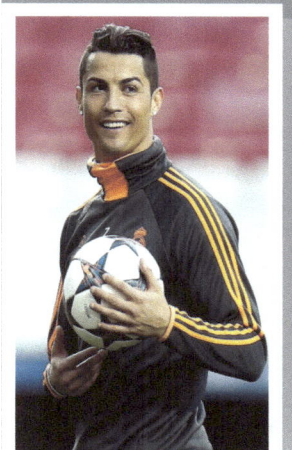

Cristiano Ronaldo,

The Portugal and Real Madrid star was voted the sport's most valuable player in the world in 2013 for the second time in his career after scoring 69 goals in 59 club and country competitions. Real Madrid rewarded him with a record 5-year contract worth more than $200 million. In May, he went on to help the team win its tenth Champions League title.

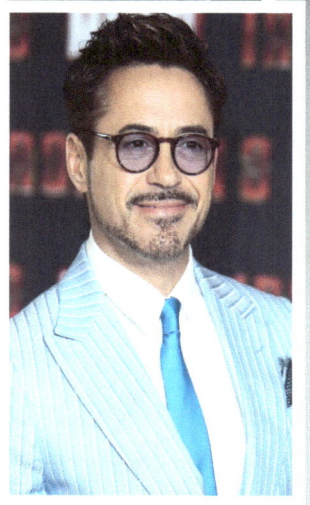

Robert Downey Jr

The Avengers was the third highest-grossing movie of all time and no star benefited more from that than Robert Downey Jr. Tony Stark might not have been the leader of the group (that honor belongs to Captain America) but Downey was the only indispensable actor which meant he was able to

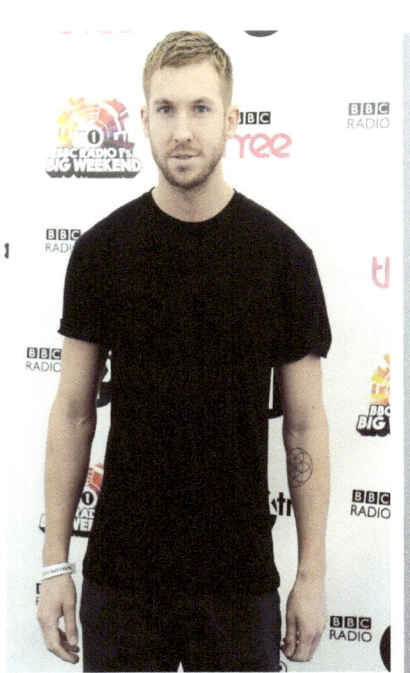

Calvin Harris

makes his debut on FORBES' Celebrity 100 after a stellar year. Discovered on Myspace eight year ago as a singer-songwriter, Harris has morphed into a world-renowned DJ and producer. In February, he signed on to play more than 70 shows over a two-year period in Las Vegas. While the majority of his money comes from performing, he also earns from writing and producing songs like Rihanna's Grammy-winning "We Found Love." Harris played more than 150 shows in the 12 months since June 1, 2012.

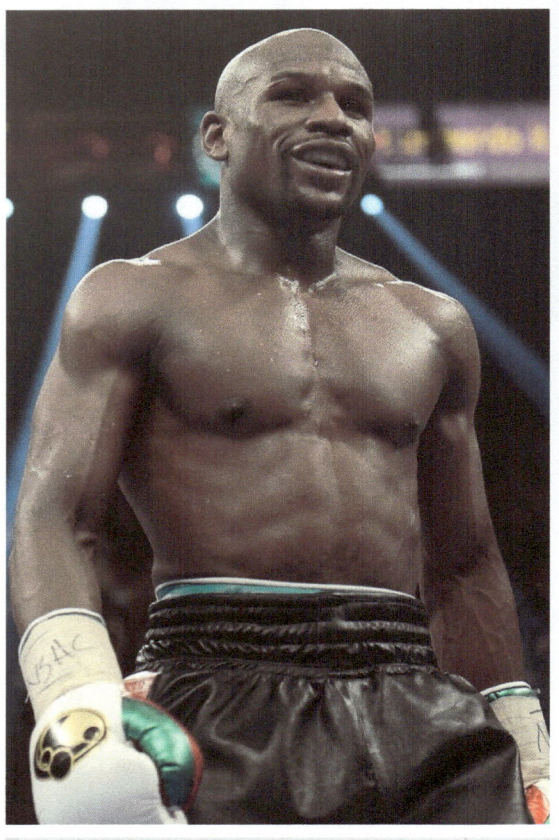

Floyd Mayweather

Mayweather is the first athlete besides Tiger Woods to earn $100 million in Forbes' annual tally of the highest-paid athletes. His September 2013 fight against Canelo Alvarez set records for highest PPV gross ($150 million), live gate ($20 million) and total revenue (roughly $200 million). The Canelo fight marked the second bout in the block-buster 30-month, six-fight deal he signed with Showtime in 2013. Mayweather earned a guaranteed $32 million for his May fight with Marcos Maidana where the PPV buys are expected to finish between 900,000 and one million when they are all counted, compared to 2.2 million for Mayweather-Alvarez. Mayweather pocketed $105 million for the two bouts thanks to his role as both pugilist and promoter.

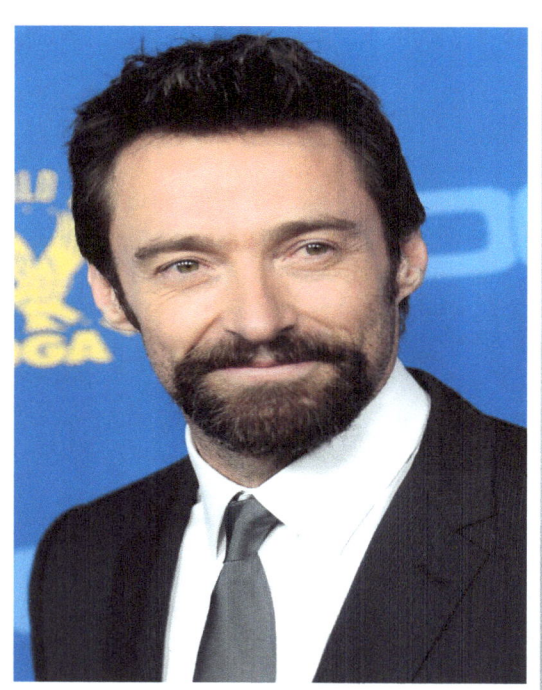

Hugh Jackman

Singing, dancing, acting, getting ripped to kick some bad guy's butt, it's all in a day's work for Jackman. The actor, who is maybe best known for playing Wolverine in the many X-Men movies, showed last year that he can also move audiences to tears. As Jean Valjean in Les Miserables he scored an Oscar nomination and helped the musical earn $438 million on a budget of $61 million. Jackman is also a budding entrepreneur. His Laughing Man coffee and tea company donates all profits to charity.

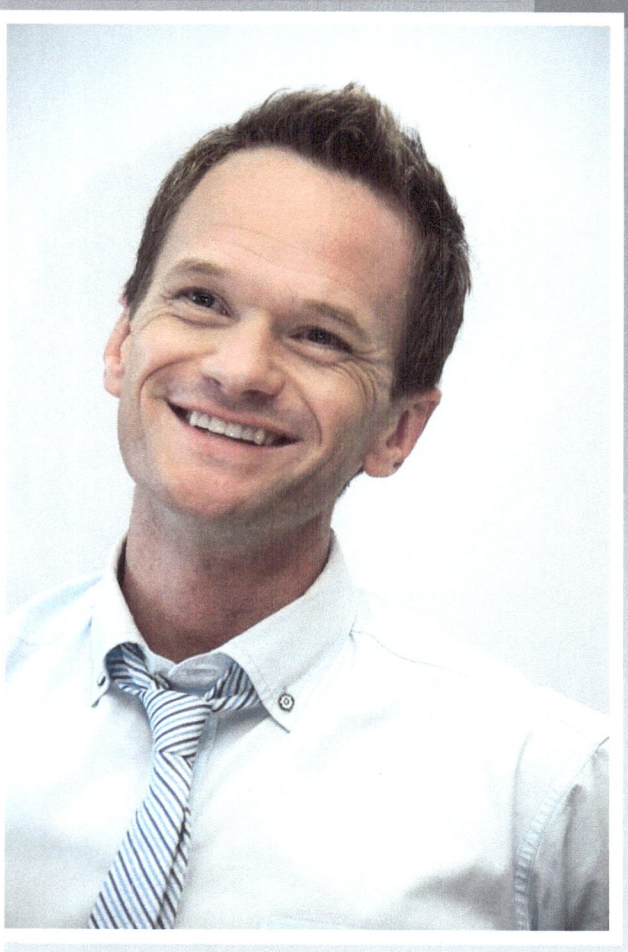

Neil Patrick Harris

The artist formerly known as Doogie Howser makes his debut on the list thanks to the huge success of How I Met Your Mother and his correspondingly growing paycheck. The upcoming ninth season of the CBS sitcom will be the show's last, but NPH need not worry: he's a triple-threat, having hoofed it on Broadway and crooned onstage as four-time host of the Tony Awards. He also makes good money off of movies like The Smurfs franchise.

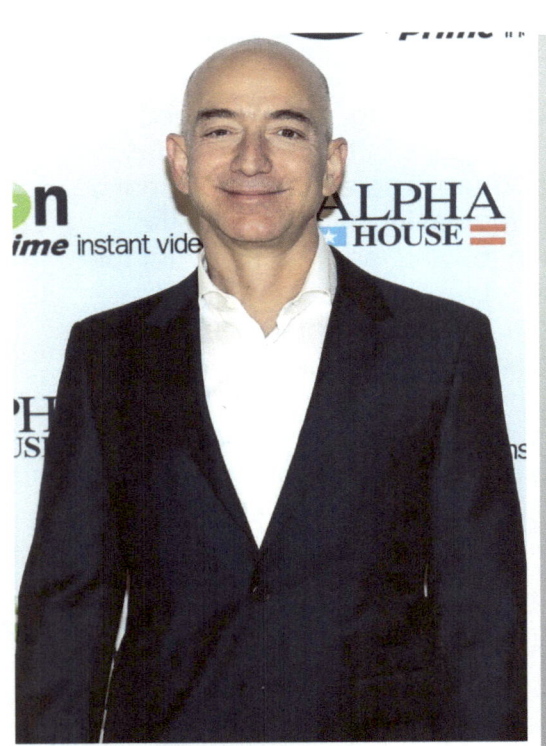

Jeff Bezos

Jeff Bezos fortune rose $13 billion in 2013 as shares in his online retailer Amazon soared 55%. In October he bought the Washington Post for $250 million. The next month he sold 1 million shares of Amazon, less than 1% of the company, for about $260 million. In December he announced that Amazon could be delivering its packages by drones within five years. After graduating with a degree in electrical engineering and computer science from Princeton, Bezos headed off to Wall Street, where he saw that the internet was the fastest-growing industry on the planet. He quit his job, headed to Seattle and founded online bookstore Amazon in 1995. The company expanded beyond books and now sells anything to anyone.

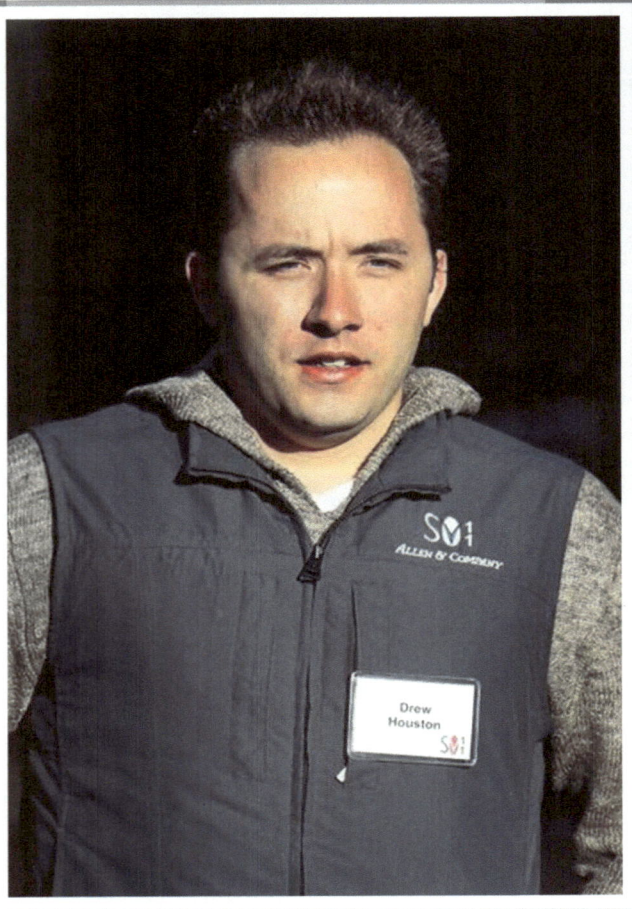

Drew Houston

Net worth: $1.2 billion Age: 30 Cofounder and CEO of Dropbox joins the club after a January funding round valued his file-sharing service at just under $10 billion, making it the most valuable private tech company in the world - and a very eligible billionaire bachelor. Houston (pronounced like the New York City street, not the Texas city) cofounded Dropbox, a cloud-based file-sharing service, with Arash Ferdowsi in 2007. Rumors abound that Dropbox plans to file for an initial public offering in 2014; Houston's stock could be on the rise.

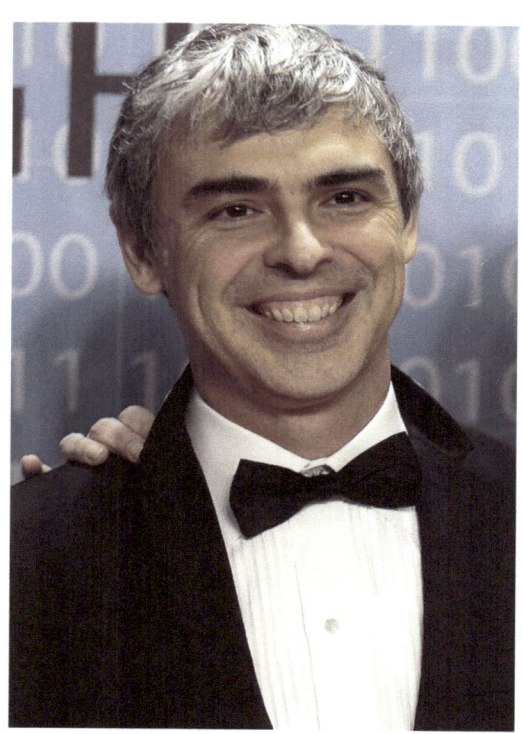

CEO Larry Page
is rearranging the furniture at Google. Over two weeks in January, he announced his company's $3.2 billion, all-cash acquisition of smart-thermostat-maker Nest as well as the $2.9 billion sale of its Motorola phone business to Lenovo. Shareholders seem happy. The search giant's stock continues to trade at record highs, up about 50% year-over-year as of mid-Feb. 2014. That's caused the net worth of co-founders Page and Sergey Brin to surge past $30 billion for the first time. In April, Google will undergo a stock split to introduce new Class C shares that will carry no voting power. That move will consolidate the voting power of executives including Page, who owns nearly 24 million Class B shares, which carry 10-to-one voting power. He's still suffering from

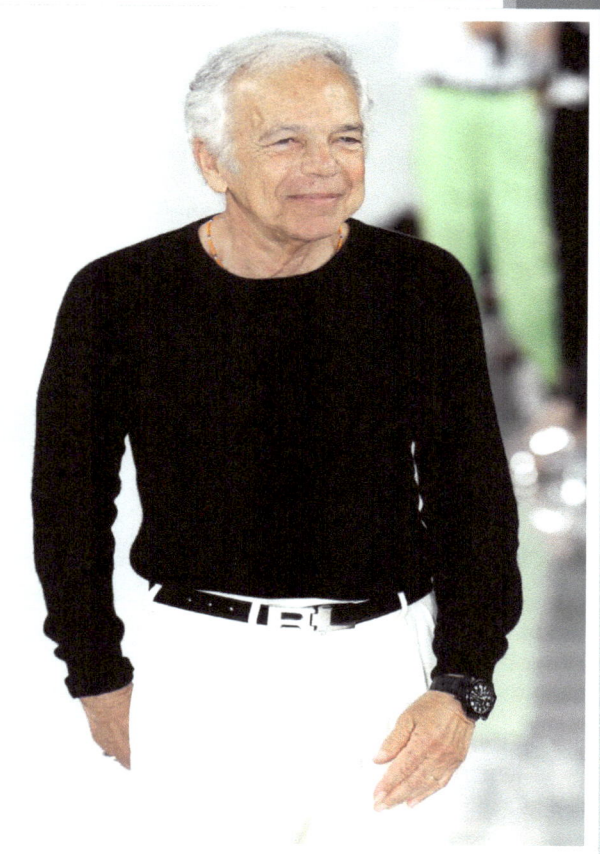

Fashion designer Ralph Lauren's Net worth is unchanged from last year. Shares of his eponymous company hit an all-time high in August before receding in early 2014. He announced the launch of Polo Ralph Lauren for Women this year during New York City's Fashion Week. His son David, who heads global advertising and marketing, recently joined the board of directors. An avid car collector, Lauren reportedly paid $1.4 million in August for LaFerrari, a hybrid supercar that can go from zero to 120mph in 7 seconds. Son of a Russian immigrant, he grew up in Bronx and worked part-time in rag trade at Alexander's from age 16. He launched Polo with a $50,000 loan in 1967 and took it public in 1997. His car collection (Bugatti, Bentley, Alfa Romeo, Ferrari) is so well regarded that Boston's Museum of Fine Arts exhibited it in 2005. Lauren has recently pledged to restore and modernize the Ecole National Superieure des

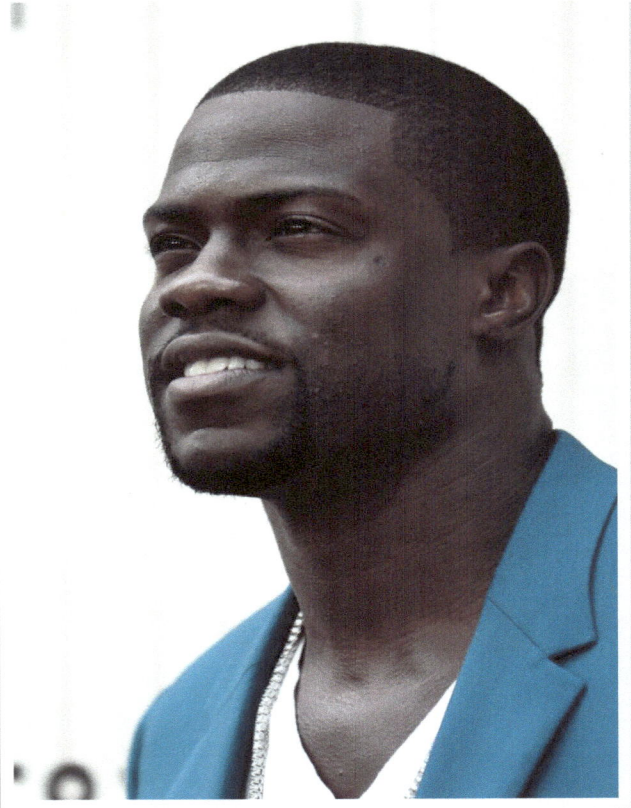

Kevin Hart

Hart's persona on his BET mock reality show Real Husbands of Hollywood is that of a man always looking to climb the ranks of Hollywood's A-list elite. Thanks to high-grossing gigs and multi-platinum sales of his DVD, Laugh at My Pain, which grossed over $8 million since its release, Hart is climbing FORBES' list as well. "Husbands" debuted to 4.1 million viewers and was picked up for a second season. The comedian is also gaining attention in Hollywood with a roster of upcoming films and recent roles in hits like Think Like A Man and This Is The End.

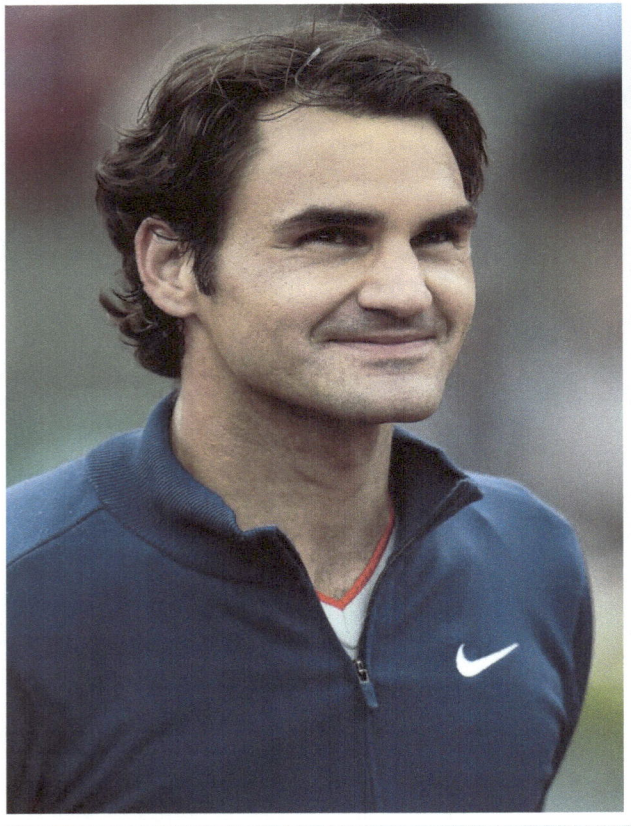

Rodger Federer

Federer continues to be among the world's best players 16 years after he turned pro. He holds the records for most singles Grand Slam wins (17) and career prize money ($81 million). He appeared in a staggering 18 out of 19 Grand Slam finals between 2005 and 2010. His endorsement portfolio is filled with long-term deals with blue-chip companies like Nike, Rolex and Credit Suisse. His sponsors collectively pay him more than $40 million annually. The latest addition is champagne brand Moet & Chandon, which signed Federer to a five-year deal at the end of 2012.

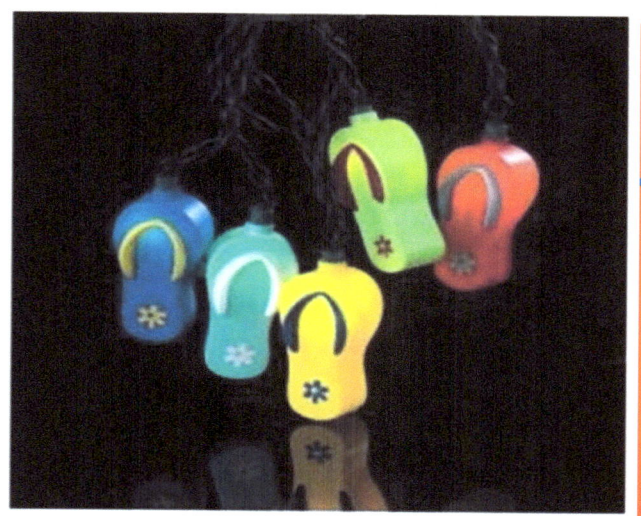

Local Business Ad for sale
See back of magazine for More information!

The World of Entertainment

TOP PICKS OF THIS MONTH.....

Hard Choices
Hillary Rodham Clinton
Hillary Rodham Clinton's inside account of the crises, choices, and challenges she faced during her four years as America's 67th Secretary of State, and how those experiences drive her view of the future.

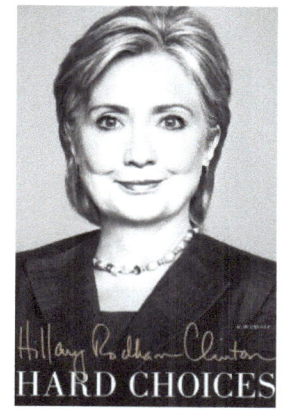

Mr. Mercedes
Stephen King
In a mega-stakes, high-suspense race against time, three of the most unlikely and winning heroes Stephen King has ever created try to stop a lone killer from blowing up thousands.

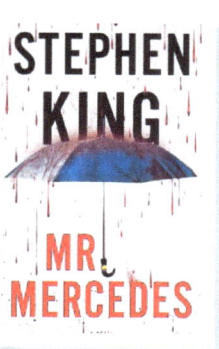

Before I fall
Lauren Oliver
Samantha Kingston has it all: the world's most crush-worthy boyfriend, three amazing best friends, and first pick of everything at Thomas Jefferson High, from the best table in the cafeteria to the choicest parking spot. Friday, February 12 should be just another day in her charmed life.
Instead, it turns out to be her last.

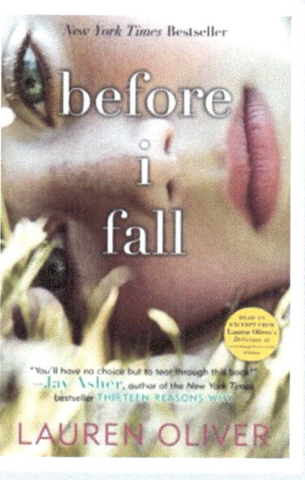

Doggy's World
Music Events:

U.S. Airways Center Presents

Marquee Theatre Presents

Phoenix Mercury VS Chicago Sky
July 2

Chevelle
July 13

WNBA All Star Event
July 19

Summerland Tour 2014 With Everclear
July 15

Lady Gaga: The ARTPOP Ball
July 30

Say Anything with The Front Bottoms, The So So Glos, You Blew It!
July 27

201 E Jefferson St. Phoenix, AZ 85004 602-379-7878

730 N Mill Ave, Tempe AZ 85281, 480-829-0607

Fashion No or not….
Brought to you by: Lisabeths Design

Men's suits, and the foreign look we like

Have you ever walked by a man in a nice suite and suddenly felt the urge to go do something French?
Well we have and yes we did go French, our men's fashions have crossed overseas and we had to prepare ourselves with fun filled facts to guide us through the French Side Of A Man!
France is known as the country of luxury, fashion and beauty, with a world's fashion capital based in Paris, but also with many cities and towns with an important history and industry of the entry, with important also large and small events and shows as fashion weeks and fests. French design became prominent during the 15th–20th centuries, when artistic development in France was at its peak. The fashion industry has been an important cultural export of France since the seventeenth century; modern haute couture originated in Paris in the 1860s. Paris acts as the center of the French fashion industry. Along with New York City, London and Milan, the city is considered one of the world's fashion capitals, housing many premier fashion designers, including, but not limited to, Pierre Cardin, Céline, Chanel, Chloe, Dior, Givenchy, Jean Paul Gaultier, Hermès, Lanvin, Rochas, Vuitton and Yves Saint Laurent
Today people like Antoine Arnault, chief executive at Berluti, and Alessandro Sartori are changing the mens fashion world. For these men they dedicated time and money to the french, italian, etc, fashions that intesise us all. Recently spending close to 350 million in Euros dedicated to mens wear company we are sure to appreciate.

Here is a few places were you can go get your french on!

1. http://www.mensitaly.com/
2. http://www.brotherstailorsaz.com/
3. http://www.menswearhouse.com/
4. http://www.macys.com
5. http://www.aliexpress.com

DESIGN SEO STYLE CREATE SEO LIFE

Creating a Buzz from your website
1. Make the Most of Social Media
Create attractive pages on all major social networks, such as Facebook, Twitter, Pinterest, Instagram, and YouTube. Load them with teasers, one-liners, quality images, and videos, as well as fun facts that are relevant to your type of business.
Add links to your website in every post you share and engage extensively with other users. Re-share their content and comment on their posts. What you are ultimately trying to do is get your audience so excited about your social media pages, that they are eager to find out more about you and look for your website.
The key here is engagement. Don't make your social pages feel like link-pushing robots. Give them a personal touch and let your followers know that there's a real person on

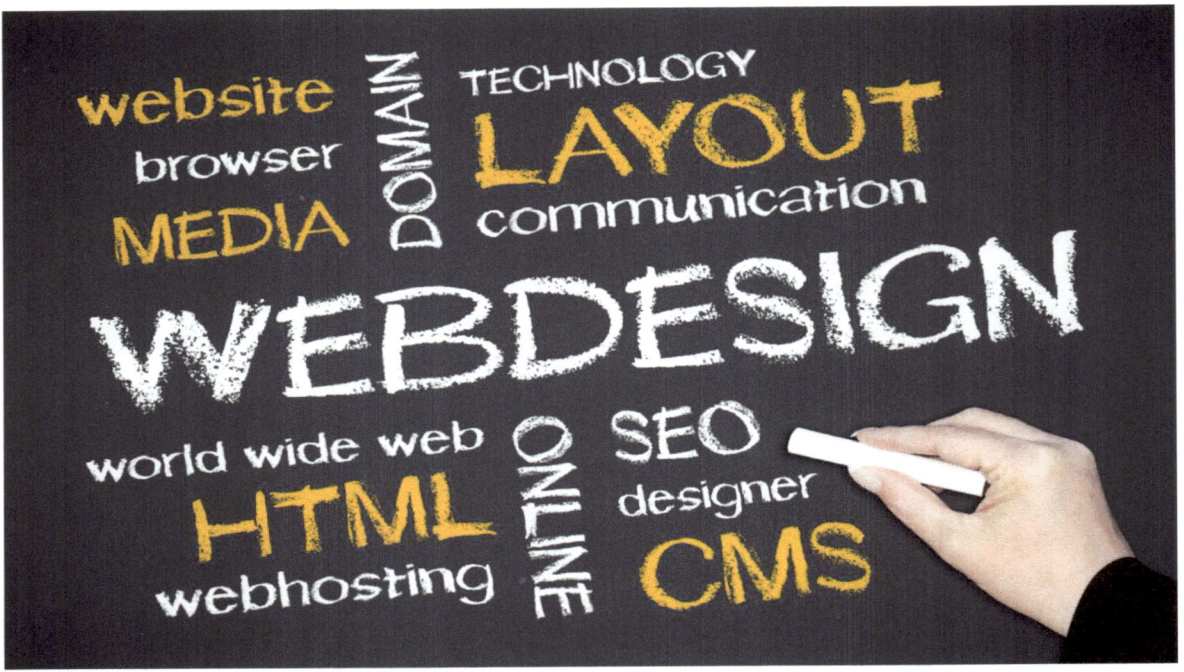

Frank's New York Style Deli

While working in the area I decided I would give Franks NY Deli a try. Pulling up I had to double check the address as Franks is located in a small neighborhood market.

The food is not deserving of the ratings here on Yelp as it is lower end processed meats and the menu is very limited with maybe 10 sandwich options. I got the NY combo which is simply salami, ham, and choice of cheese. The sandwich is on a 10" roll and you get the basic toppings of lettuce, tomato, onion, and dressings. The sandwich and a 16.9oz beverage was $6.45 which is a fair price for what you get.

Customer Reviews.........

Coming from NY, this place hit close to home. This place is a family-owned business and the place has got some character.   They definitely reminded me of the delis in NY.   The subs are out of this world!!!
Why bother going to subway where they give you like three slices of meat and one slice of cheese when you can get the most amazing subs at Frank's Deli. I love the Italian sub and the meatball sub. mmmhmmmm. I could go for some right now. The rice pudding is my favorite dessert, but they do have pretty good cheesecake too. :)

Customer Reviews...........

Located At:

2301 W Orange Dr.
Phoenix, AZ 85015

602-242-8288

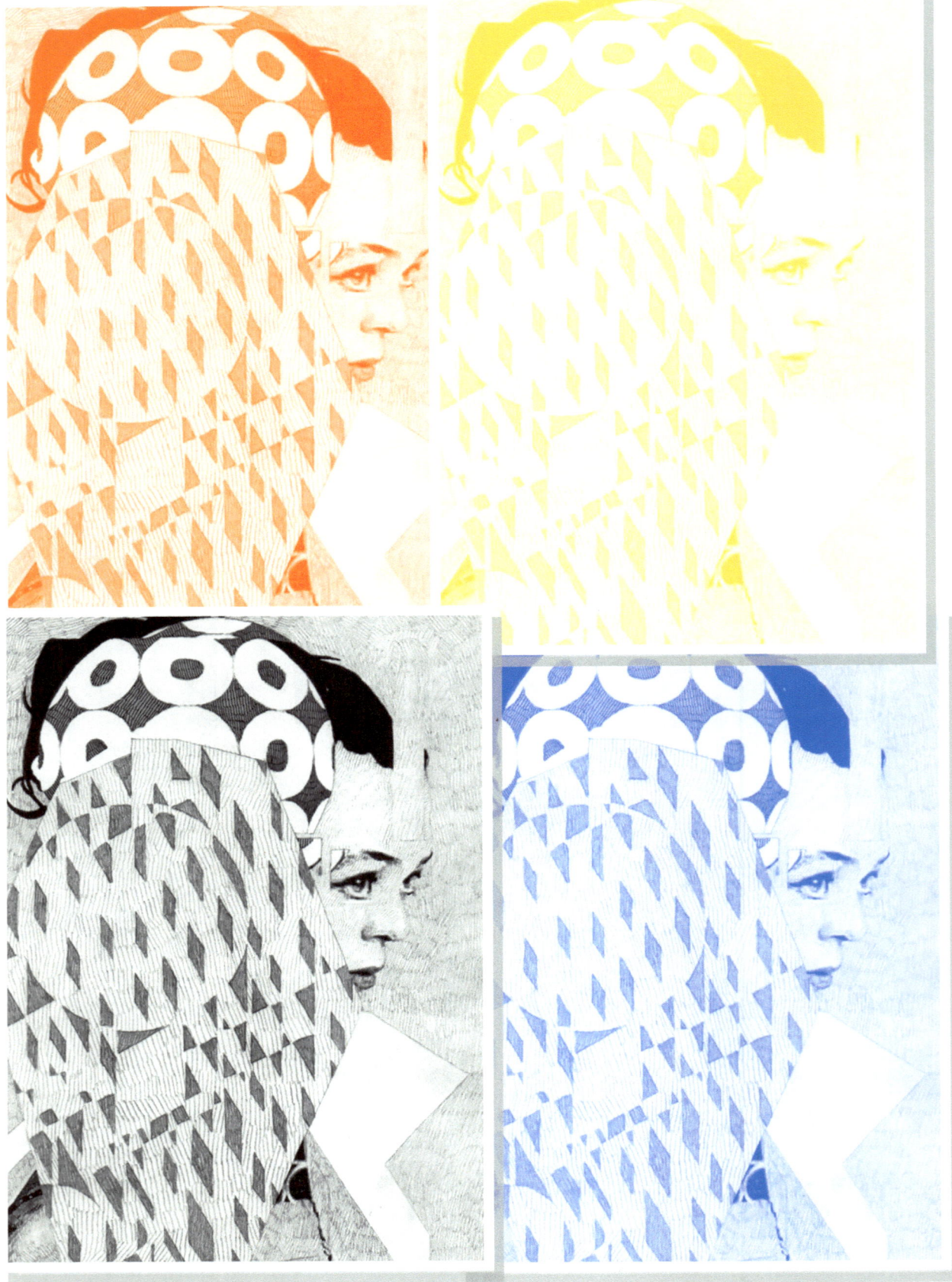

French-speaking painters continued the Mannerist conventions even later than did those at Haarlem, and at Nancy (capital of the independent duchy of Lorraine before 1633 and again from 1697 to 1766) a group of artists around Jacques Bellange and Jacques Callot was responsible for the last great flowering of the Mannerist style in Europe. By comparison, painting in Paris during the first decades of the 17th century was relatively insignificant, with the exception of that of Claude Vignon, who exchanged his Mannerist training for a style based on Elsheimer and to a lesser extent Lastman, and who in the 1620s revealed a remarkable knowledge of the earliest paintings of Rembrandt. The return of Simon Vouet to Paris, however, marked the arrival of the Baroque in France. The earliest paintings from his stay in Rome are strikingly vigorous essays in the Caravaggesque style, but by 1620 he was painting in an eclectic, classicizing style based on the early Baroque painters active there, including Giovanni Lanfranco and Guido Reni. This style he brought back to France, enjoying until his death an immense success in Paris as a decorator and painter of large-scale altarpieces; even the return of Nicolas Poussin failed to shake his position. Poussin's activity in Paris is of relatively little importance compared with the remainder of his career in Rome, but the large number of works commissioned by French patrons then and subsequently was an important factor in the formation of the French predilection for classicism. Another Frenchman, Claude Lorrain in Rome, had his sources in the romantic landscapes of the late Mannerists. By 1640 he established an international reputation. Both Poussin and Claude had been formed in Rome, but they remained typically French with a spiritual seriousness subjugated entirely to the laws of reason.

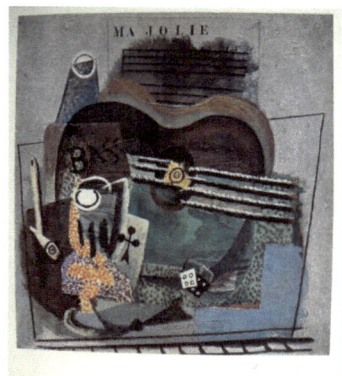
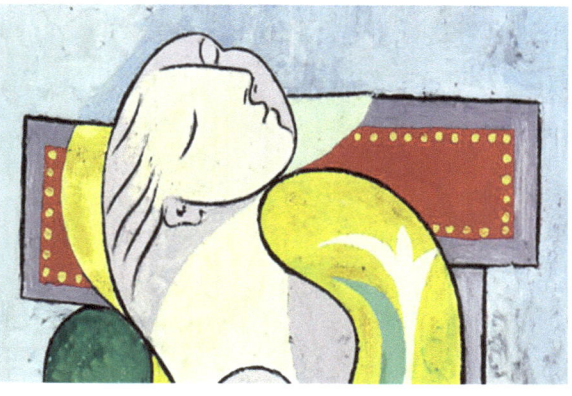
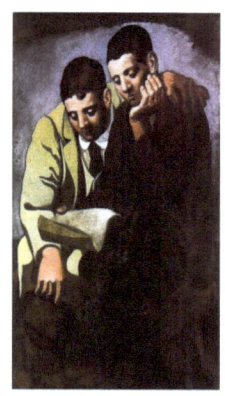

Trendy News What You Want To Know

Rupert Grint Hits Broadway!

Rupert Grint, best known for playing Ron Weasley in the block-buster "Harry Potter" film franchise, will make his Broadway debut this fall in Terrence McNally's starry comedy It's Only a Play. Grint joins an A-list cast that includes Matthew Broderick, Nathan Lane, Stockard Channing, Megan Mullally, F. Murrary Abraham and newcomer Micah Stock. Jack O'Brien will direct the limited 17-week engagement, which opens at Broadway's Schoenfeld Theatre on October 9

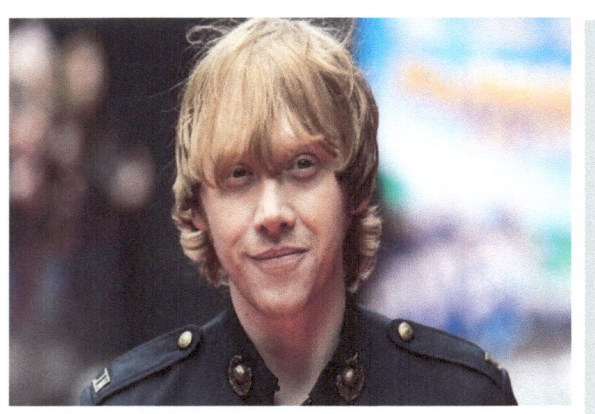
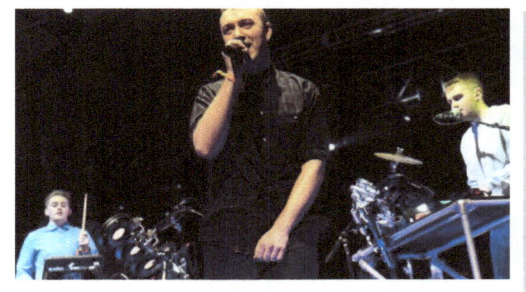

Sam Smith. Reviews on new Album

Sam Smith new album gets reviews from Rolling Stone, were excited to see new material from him. In his interview he admits to dedicateding his album to his "love." He said, " With In the Lonely Hour's orchestral flourishes and focus on a single unrealized affair, it seems the baby-faced singer is being positioned as a male Adele. But while the album flirts with a few radiant moments, Smith's endless yearning isn't wrapped in as many irresistible packages. " Rolling Stone.

New Technology For The Modern Geek

The Berowatch Air W2: A Smart Watch For All Android phones

The BeroWatch Air is compatible with all Android devices. This impeccably designed watch has a variety of features that beats all the other smart watches on the market. Unlike the Pebble Smart Watch, this watch has a built in speaker and can send and receive calls straight from your watch via a low-energy Bluetooth connection. The built-in, high-powered speaker and mic allows you to have phone conversations straight from the watch without ever having to take out your phone. You don't even have to hold the watch up to your mouth, the mic is so strong that it acts like a Bluetooth speaker, only difference is it is strapped to your wrist!

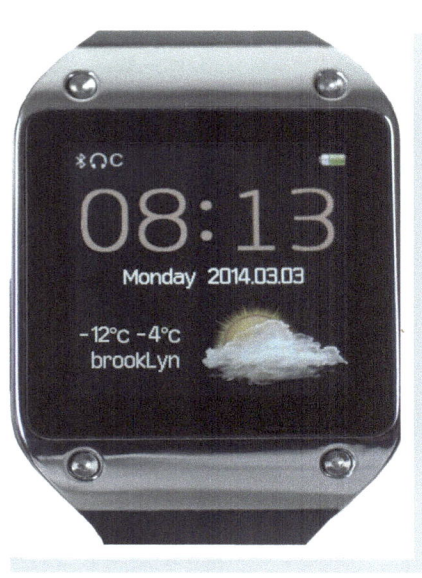

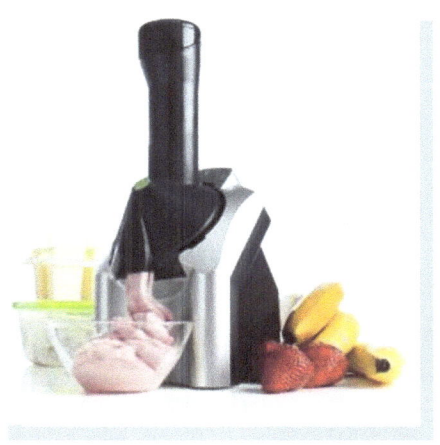

Yonanas 901 Deluxe Ice Cream Treat Maker, Black/Silver

Made in USA or Imported

Yonanas instantly turns frozen fruit and other flavorings into a delicious and healthy soft-serve treat.

The unit instantly churns the ingredients to produce a treat with the texture of frozen yogurt or soft-serve ice cream

The chute easily accepts berries, sliced mango, or cantaloupe along with frozen banana to incorporate the fruit into a silky-smooth confection

New Technology Vs. The other guys

Technological development has providedhuman history with a kind of directionality All of the biggest technological inventions created by man - the airplane, theautomobile, the computer - says little about his intelligence, but speaksvolumes about his laziness. Mark Kennedy Humanity or Mankind has evolved fromthe essence that separates humans from beasts:the ability to use the mind for reason. Reason isthe ability to analyze, create, deduce, andformulate. It is reason that enables human beingsto strive to invent; it is through invention thatmankind has developed society and created abetter world.we could say that technology is the sumtotal of instrumentally useful culturally-transmissible information.Technology, a word with Greek origins,
is defined as, "the practical application
of knowledge e
specially in a particular area"
.Technology is a word used to collectivelydescribe or portray the advancements, abilities,creations, undertakings, views, and knowledgeof a singular group of persons: we as human-kind. Little by little, Internet and mobile technology seems to be subtly destroying the meaningfulness of interactions we have with others, disconnecting us from the world around us, and leading to an imminent sense of isolation in today's society. Instead of spending time in person with friends, we just call, text or instant message them. It may seem simpler, but we ultimately end up seeing our friends face to face a lot less. Ten texts can't even begin to equal an hour spent chatting with a friend over lunch. And a smiley-face emoticon is cute, but it could never replace the ear-splitting grin and smiling eyes of one of your best friends. Face time is important, people. We need to see each other.

Sensory dynamism

Enhancement

Human enhancement refers to any attempt to temporarily or permanently overcome the current limitations of the human body through natural or artificial means. The term is sometimes applied to the use of technological means to select or alter human characteristics and capacities, whether or not the alteration results in characteristics and capacities that lie beyond the existing human range. Here, the test is whether the technology

In scientific usage, a phenomenon is any event that is observable, however common it might be, even if it requires the use of instrumentation to observe, record, or compile data concerning it. For example, in physics, a phenomenon may be a feature of matter, energy, or space-time, such as Isaac Newton's observations of the moon's orbit and of gravity, or Galileo Galilee's observations of the motion of a pendulum.[4] Another example of scientific phenomena can be found in the experience of phantom limb sensations. This occurrence, the sensation of feeling in amputated limbs, is reported by over 70% of amputees. Although the limb is no longer present, they report still experiencing sensations. This is an extraordinary event that defies typical logic and has been a source of much curiosity within the medical and physiological fields

In recent decades, a new possibility for LGBT parenting, same-sex procreation (where two women could have a daughter with equal genetic contributions from both women, or where two men could have a son or daughter with equal genetic contributions from both men), has become a possibility, through the creation of either female sperm or male eggs from the cells of adult women and men. With female sperm and male eggs, lesbian and gay couples wishing to become parents would not have to rely on a third party donor of sperm or egg.

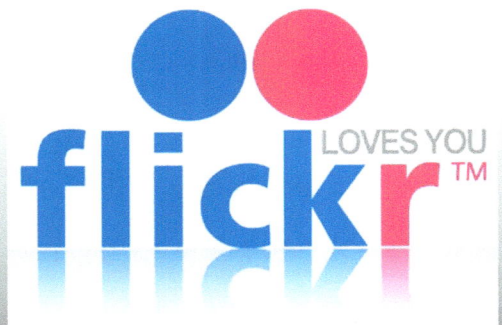

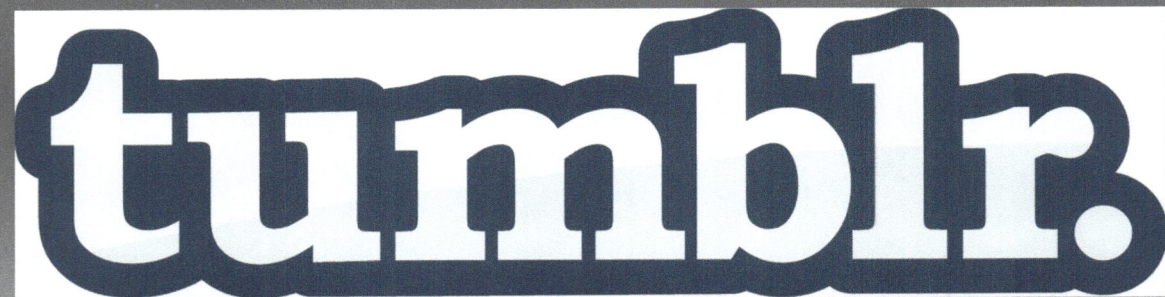

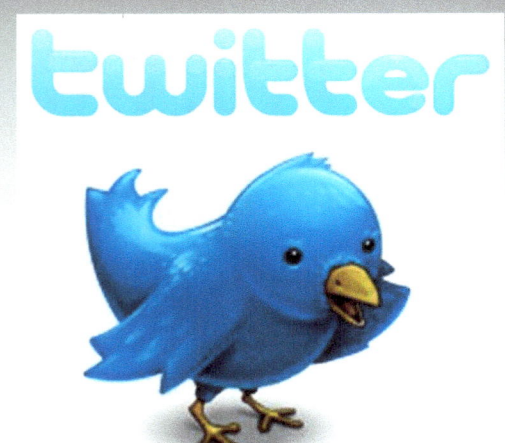

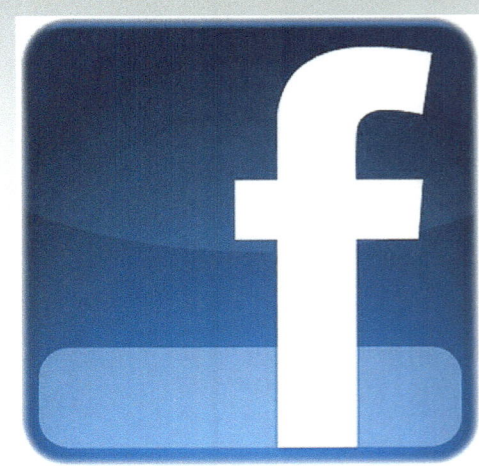

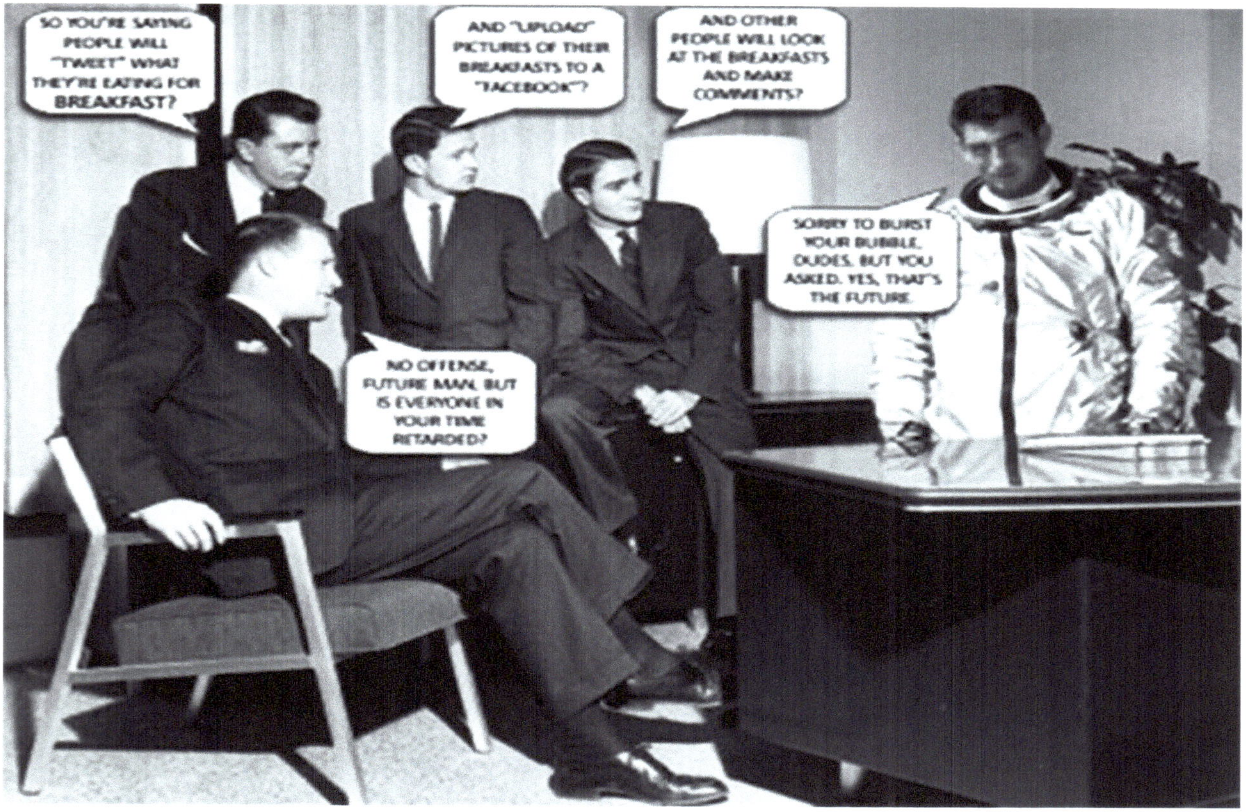

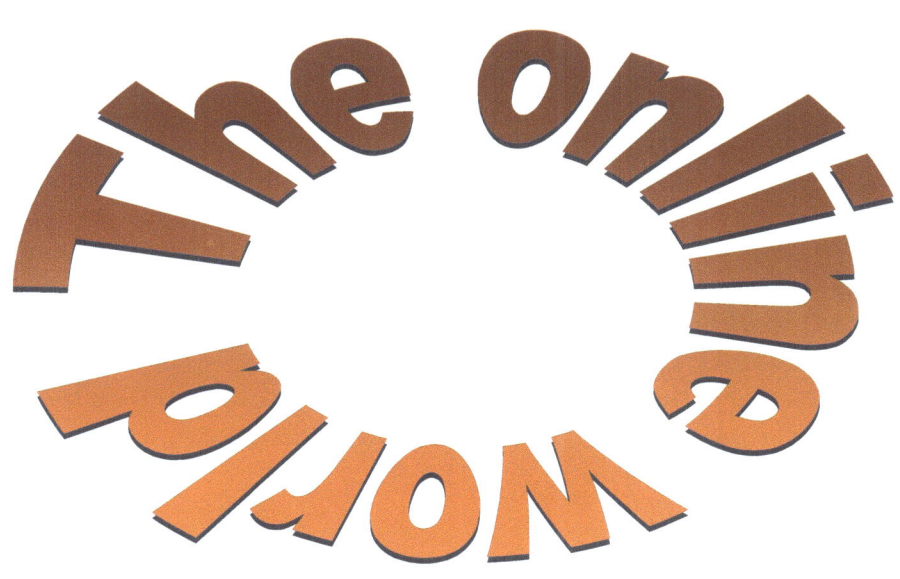

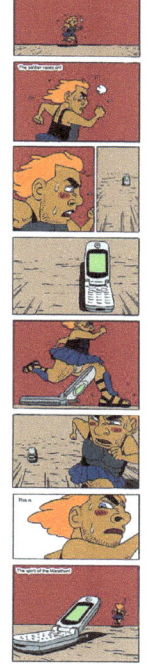

Business Watch: What We Need To Know

Joint Chiefs chairman: Iraq has asked for U.S. air power to counter militants

While Iraq's military claimed Wednesday to have driven back militants battling for control of the country, the chairman of the Joint Chiefs of Staff told Congress that the United States has received a request from the Iraqi government to use its air power in the conflict. U.S. embassy on alert in Iraq

Sunni Deputy PM: We are isolated

Atta claimed that Iraq's military were "defeating ISIS in the Baiji area" and that "most of the areas" around the northwestern city of Tal Afar were liberated.

That apparently included 50 Siemens employees, including eight Germans, who were holed up in a power station in Baiji but have been freed, according to German officials. The employees are safe and well, CNN was told.

According to German diplomats, around 8,000 German nationals are currently in Iraq.

Tal Afar fell to ISIS on Sunday, according to Iraq's military. Many Tal Afar residents, including ethnic minority Shiite Turkmen, fled the fighting north toward Iraq's Kurdish region.

How Jimmy Graham's Twitter Bio Could Cost Him $5M

Unable to reach a long-term contract extension with the New Orleans Saints, superstar Jimmy Graham is at an identity-crisis crossroads. The Saints are keen on slapping Graham with the franchise tag, which would lock him in to a one-year contract worth maximum dollar value for his position. But whether the massive pass-catcher should be considered a tight end or a wide receiver is a big determinant in how he will be paid in 2014.

Hillary Clinton and understanding Immigration

Hillary Clinton wants Americans to believe that she made difficult decisions as secretary of state. That's the premise of her new book, "Hard Choices." Somehow, I suspect that if Clinton had a do-over for this week's CNN town hall, she might choose not to field a hard question from Francisco Gonzalez. A professor at the Paul H. Nitze School of Advanced International Studies at Johns Hopkins University, Gonzales asked America's former top diplomat about President Obama's record of removing the undocumented and splitting up families with such efficiency that, as Gonzales noted, many Hispanics call Obama the "deported in chief." He asked what Clinton would do differently.– cnn sourced

Survive The Realestate Market

Paying A Bonus To The Broker?
Question: Our home has been listed for sale for several months. Early on our real estate agent hosted an open house for real estate agents and brokers. At this meeting, someone suggested to our agent that we should offer a bonus to the selling agent. Afterward our agent pushed this idea with us stating that "with the bonus our house would go to the top of the list for showing and without a bonus we would get no action". I considered this blackmail and refused the idea. We have had only one showing since that time. What is your opinion about the ethics of this practice?

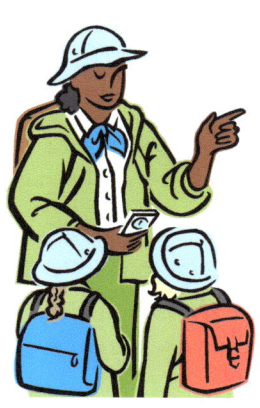

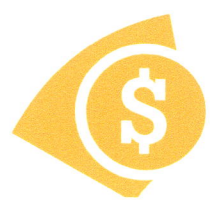

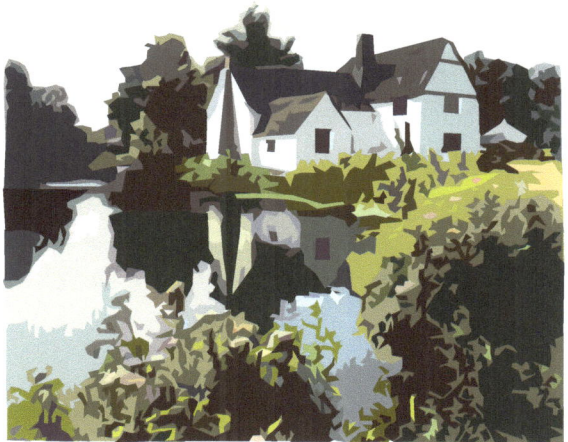

Politics: Special Feature

Obama : Foreign Policy
It's a new low for President Barack Obama.

Facing numerous international challenges, including the new blood-shed in Iraq, the civil war in Syria, and the fighting in Ukraine, as well as the controversial swapping of five Taliban prisoners held at Guantanamo Bay for the release of a U.S. soldier held captive in Afghanistan, a new NBC News/Wall Street Journal poll indicates just 37% of Americans say they approve of how the President's handling foreign policy. That's an all time low in NBC News/Wall Street Journal polling.

House GOP leaders: Keep Iran out of the mix in Iraq
Ahead of a White House meeting Wednesday, House Speaker John Boehner called on President Barack Obama to lay out a "broader strategy" for how to deal with sectarian violence in Iraq, but the Ohio Republican said the United States should "absolutely not" talk to Iranians about the crisis.

"I can just imagine what our friends in the region, our allies will be thinking by reaching out to Iran at a time when they continue to pay for terrorists and foster terrorism not only in Syria, in Lebanon but in Israel as well," Boehner told reporters after the House GOP weekly conference meeting.

Shooting of 2 priests was burglary gone bad; suspect arrested, Phoenix police say
A suspect arrested in last week's deadly shooting at a Catholic church admitted "involvement in the crime" while in custody, Phoenix Police Chief Daniel V. Garcia said Monday.

One priest died in the shooting and another was seriously wounded. The suspect, Gary Michael Moran, was identified through DNA evidence recovered both at the crime scene and from a car stolen from the church, Garcia said at a news conference. Witnesses also came forth with information, he added.

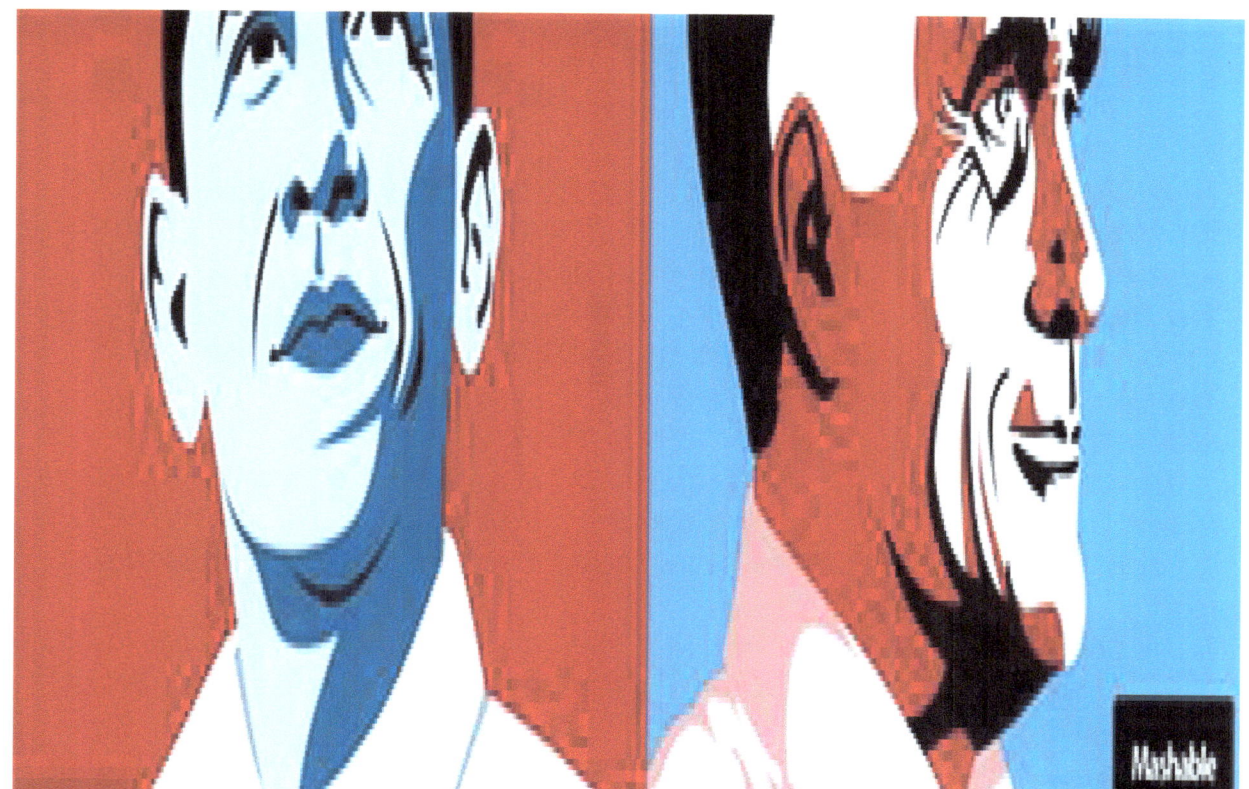

Politics Transformed

THE HIGH-TECH BATTLE FOR YOUR VOTE

Politics: The who and what of Politics

Odin Lloyd's death, loved ones cling to memories and pain

For Ursula Ward, visiting her son's gravesite has become a painful yet inescapable part of her daily routine.

"He touched our lives so much," she said.

A year ago Father's Day would be the last time they spoke.

"See you later," she told him.

Inside the case against Aaron Hernandez

In the early hours of June 17, 2013, Odin Lloyd was gunned down near a pile of construction waste in an industrial park. He was 27.

His body, shot seven times, was found the next afternoon by a jogger.

Father of Oregon school shooter: 'We are at a loss'

The father of 15-year-old Jared Padgett does not understand what compelled his son to open fire at his Oregon school.

Padgett killed one student this week at Reynolds High School in Troutdale, about 12 miles east of Portland. He also injured a teacher, before turning the gun on himself.

"I, Michael Padgett and my ex-wife, Kristina, are grieved in our hearts for the tragic event that involved our beloved son Jared at Reynolds High School.

Cops: Mom thought hubby cheated, so she killed kids

Did mom gas kids to death to get back at hubby?

Did mom gas kids to death to get back at hubby?

A 29-year-old mother was charged with two counts of first degree murder for the death of her two young children in a horrifying incident that occurred last Thursday.

The New York Post reports sources told them Lissette Bamenga fed her children juice spiked with a de-icer, and then sealed the apartment's windows with plastic before turning on the kitchen stove gas burners. Sources allegedly told The New York Post that Bamenga believed her husband had gotten another woman pregnant, so she allegedly killed their children to punish him. Bamenga allegedly slit her wrists in an attempt to commit suicide but she survived, according to reports from The New York Post.

2014 JULY

SUNDAY	MONDAY	TUESDAY	WEDNESDAY	THURSDAY	FRIDAY	SATURDAY
		1	2	3	4	5
6	7	8	9	10	11	12
13	14	15	16	17	18	19
20	21	22	23	24	25	26
27	28	29	30	31		

This month will be a great month!
July will spice things up!

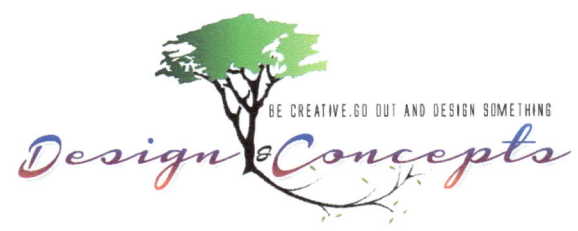

Join our mailing list and get a free 1 month Subscription to our magazine!
www.lisabethdesignmagazine.com

Owner
Design & Concepts L.L.C
Elizabeth Chavez
602-785-1108

Creativedesignconcepts@rocketmail.com

Place orders by email or contact

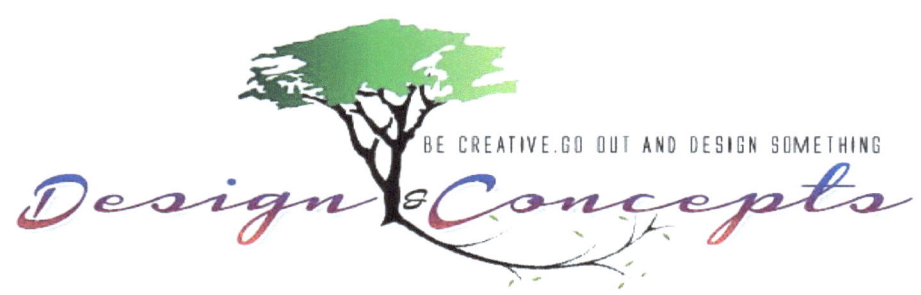

BE CREATIVE.GO OUT AND DESIGN SOMETHING

House of Lisabeths Design Magazine
We were started in 2013 as an independent magazine. Our focus is fashion, health and business. We pride ourselves in the design and diversity we offer.
Exclusivity
Our focus is fashion , health and business. Our fashion section includes tips and trends from all over! We also have a online blog that gets tons of clicks per day, check us out online at ......
Our business section is used for local or national business to place a Ad or listing of them selfs. We have total exclusivity In that they connect with not only our magazine but all of our networks simultaneously.
Our hope is to reach across the world along with Water 4 Kids International.
We plan to donate proceeds to this foundation. Our hope is to provide safe water for east Africa.
Check us out on line, Facebook, Twitter, Tumblr, Amazon, and our affiliates websites like Design & Concepts.

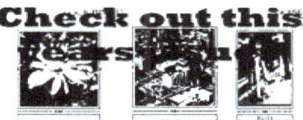

Get a 1 year subscription for $ 35.00————————— ▢
—

Get a 2 Year Subscription for $ 45.00————————— ▢
—

Payment Enclosed————————————- ▢

Charge My Card———————————— ▢

Pay Later——————————————————- ▢

Send To:

Design & Concepts
32 e Ruth Ave # 304
Phoenix, Arizona 85020

We also take check, cash and money orders.

Remember when you send for a subscription you get a free t-shirt that says "Lisabeth Design"

Thanks for supporting our fashion blog and Section!

<u>Personal Info</u>

Name:
_____

Address:
_____
_____

City, State, Zip:
_____
_____

Credit Card Info:
  Visa ▢
Master- ▢ Card
AMEX ▢

Card Number:
_____

Expiration Date:
_____

3 number code:
_____

" Fill out above info and return to address given"

Also with your subscription get a free Lisabeth Design T- Shirt

Available for Men and Women

Check out Design & Concepts Blog

Taking new ideas and turning them into key effective and business working matron for your enterprise then most likely that's what your doing now.

As far as media vs print you can see how much of a low cost each has. Similar in certain online groups were we can upload and advertise for free. Key word is always good when working these types of groups you have to remember key words. Lots of web pages will give you the minimu that's were we go in and really find specifics of what it is you do.

To be clear.........

Jane the executive director for Gumbi Gum is wanting to place a new product and have it be presented and marketed to fit a certain time frame.

Next we aske well how is the company receptive to alternative media vs the norm?

There intrigued.....

It's easy to see that by simply tacking the newer ideas and combing capability and interaction we can overcome many demanding questions.

Traditional key words and phrases are always used, used

Join the Cause!
Check out the " Design for Sick Kids Campaign'

Our Mission
In the beginning we wanted a way to show our passion for design. But this project is turning to be more then that. With so many sick kids and so much that we can give we thought about giving the gift of design.

What We Need & What You Get
Here is what we need
1000 cards , either designed by you or who ever
A contribution as well to our campaign

The Impact
With every card made we will donate a dollar and that card to a local hospital of our choice. So think about all the kids you can help by creating there Christmas card or birthday card and also the contributions that come with it.
Remember every card made we donate $ 1.00 to the cause
Also share your design with the people and get your picture taken with the kids

Other Ways You Can Help Check out our websites
www.designandconcepts.net for more updates on more causes!

http://www.indiegogo.com/projects/design-a-card-for-your-kids/

Also with your subscription get a free Lisabeth Design T- Shirt

Available for Men and Women

Design & Concepts Services

Www.Designandconcepts.net
Www.lisabethdesignmagazine.com

Design & Concepts is an online service provider for design and advertising. We specialize in brochures logos and business cards as well as t shirts and sickies. We also do local advertising with in the community. Our prices vary with design but...

Our packages start at $55.00 per package!
Package includes : 200 prints
Gloss or matt finish is $10.00 per set/ per 200

Our Packages also include our Marketing Services, and Discounts on our Advertising Specials in our magazine, House of Lisabeth De-

Also with your subscription get a free Lisabeth Design T- Shirt

Available for Men and Women

Design & Concepts Services:

Create various ads and place it on all social networks, web pages and create you tube videos to sell, demonstrate and promote your product

Also place your ad on any media source that is available We can take your campaign and place it on any other media resources you have available not just create a web presence awareness but really hit the market.

We use digital media like

Email marketing, social network campaigns, print distribution, custom Web Design and SEO

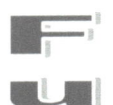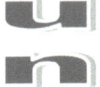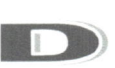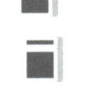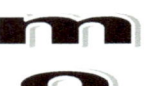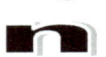

Funny Definition of the month

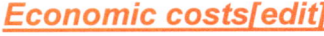

Economic costs[edit]

The economic costs of managing waste are high, and are often paid for by municipal governments;[10] money can often be saved with more efficiently designed collection routes, modifying vehicles, and with public education. Environmental policies such as pay as you throw can reduce the cost of management and reduce waste quantities. Waste recovery (that is, recycling, reuse) can curb economic costs because it avoids extracting raw materials and often cuts transportation costs. "Economic assessment of municipal waste management systems – case studies using a combination of life cycle assessment (LCA) and life cycle costing (LCC)". Journal of Cleaner Production 13 (2005): 253-263.</ref> The location of waste treatment and disposal facilities often has an impact on property values due to noise, dust, pollution, unsightliness, and negative stigma. The informal waste sector consists mostly of waste pickers who scavenge for metals, glass, plastic, textiles, and other materials and then trade them for a profit. This sector can significantly alter or reduce waste in a particular system, but other negative economic effects come with the disease, poverty, exploitation, and abuse of its workers

"Wastes are materials that are not prime products (that is products produced for the market) for which the initial user has no further use in terms of his/her own purposes of production, transformation or consumption, and of which he/she wants to dispose. Wastes may be generated during the extraction of raw materials, the processing of raw materials into intermediate and final products, the consumption of final products, and other human activities. Residuals recycled or reused at the place of generation are excluded

Recipe Of The Month

Grilled Salmon Steaks

Ingredients

4 salmon steaks 1-inch thick
1 teaspoon whole cumin seed
1 teaspoon whole coriander seed
1/2 teaspoon whole fennel seed
1 teaspoon dry green peppercorns
Sea salt or kosher salt
Canola or olive oil to coat steaks

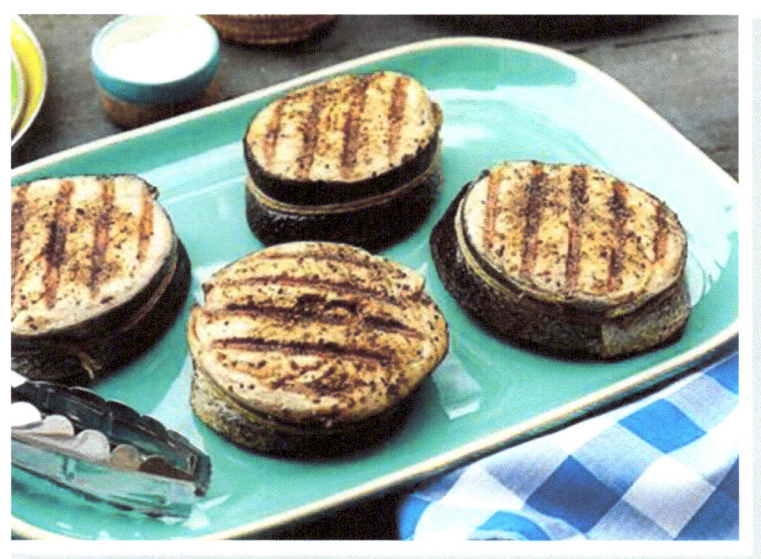

Directions

Prepare grill by lighting 4 quarts of charcoal (1 starter chimney's worth), or turning gas grill to medium-high.

Examine steaks for pin bones by rubbing fingers over surface of meat. If found, remove with bone tweezers or pliers reserved for culinary uses.

Using a sharp paring or boning knife, trim bones from the cavity side of the steak. Trim the stomach flaps so that 1 side is missing about 2 inches of skin and the other, 1 inch of meat. Roll the skinless section up into the hollow of the cavity, then wrap the other around the outside to form a round resembling a filet mignon. Tie in place with 2 passes of butcher's twine. (Do not tie it too tight or fish will pop out during cooking.)

Combine cumin, coriander, fennel and peppercorns on a double thick piece of aluminum foil and toast over grill, shaking gently until seeds become fragrant. Crush seeds in mortar and pestle or pour into spare pepper grinder. Coat steaks lightly with oil, season with salt, then liberally grind toasted seeds on both sides of steaks.

Quickly wipe hot grill grate with a rag or towel dipped in a little Canola oil, then grill fish to medium rare, about 3 minutes per side. (Fish should be well colored on the outside and barely translucent at the center.

Serve steaks alongside simple salad dressed with "Veni, Vedi, Vinaigrette."

Looking for classifieds, if interested submit your business and information and well help you out!

Liz:
creativedesignconcepts@rocketmail.com

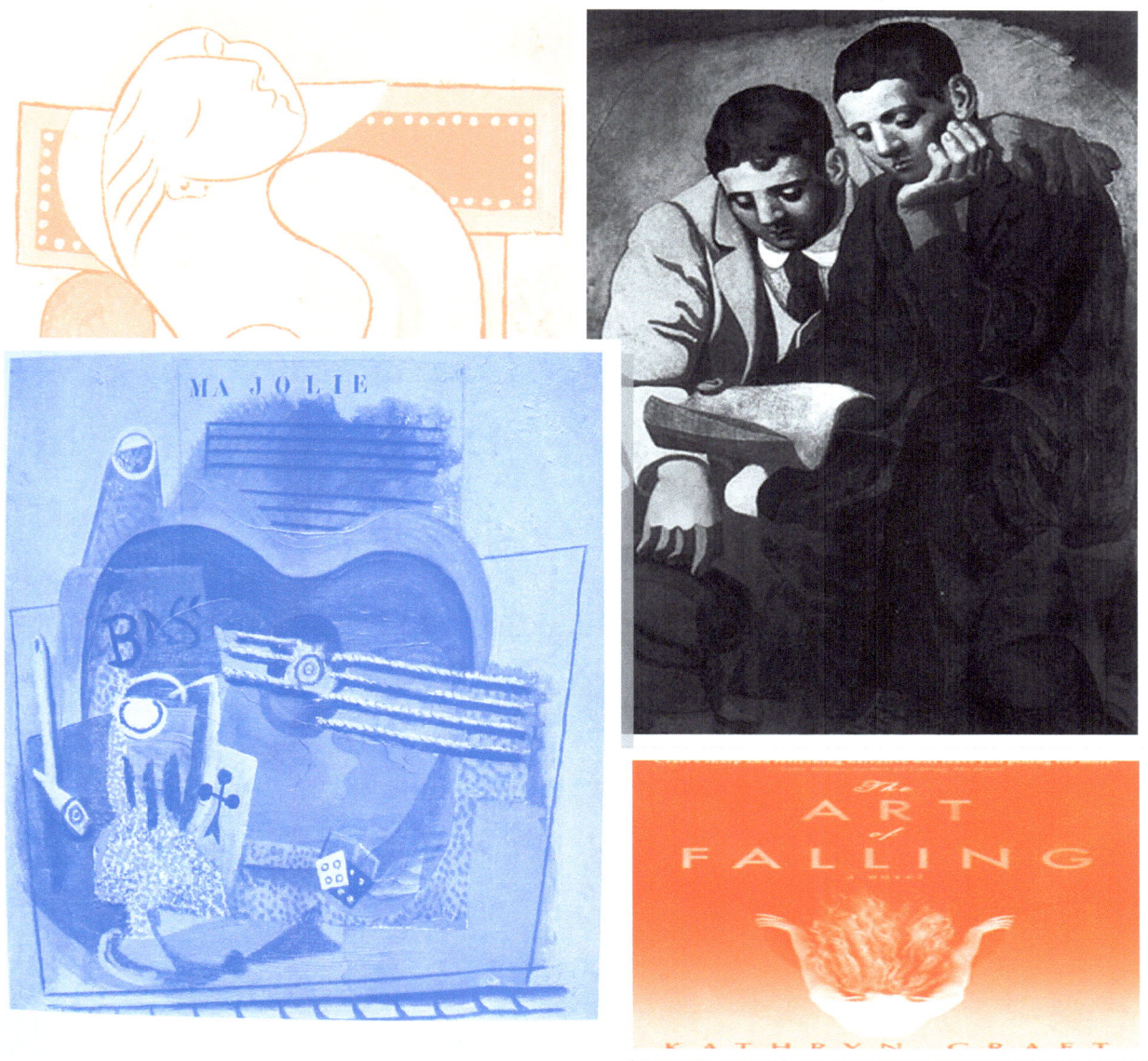

Meet The Editor and Owner.......

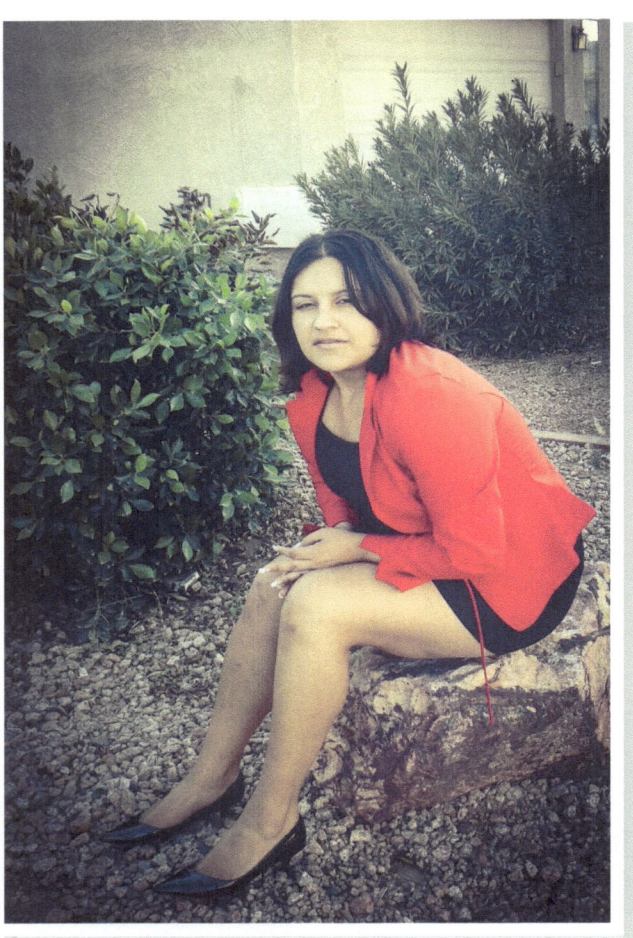

Elizabeth Chavez 27, currently the owner of Design & Concepts LLC , and editor of House of Lisabeth Design Magazine. As an entrepreneur in her own field she manages both her business and love of designing in her everyday life. She works hard by involving all things that she can in many projects that she is involved with. One of her favorite is the Design For Kids Campaign, for her this is not only about kids but about love of the community.

Classifieds

Staffmark
Call Center Training Designer
Staffmark is currently seeking TWO Training Course Designer for one of our largest clients who provides environment solutions all across the US. This is a temp-to-hire position that will start out lasting approximately 4-6 months, with a chance for the employee to be hired on permanently based on their performance in the role.

www.satffmark.com

TeleTech

Customer Service Reps
In this position, you'll be providing customer support and resolution for mid-to-high level issues which may range from enhanced roadside assistance to crash notification support. You will be empowered to solve simple to complex issues for these customers. As a TeleTech Customer Service Associate, you get to hear the personal satisfaction from your customer after you've been able to help.

www.teletech.com/careers

Vector Marketing
Entry Level Sales/ Customer Service
If you're the kind of person who has a great attitude and can succeed when given the proper training and support, then we want to hear from you. Our sales representatives present Cutco to both new and existing customers on a low-key, one-on-one basis. We offer a minimum base pay so representatives don't feel pressured to make a sale - instead they focus on providing excellent service to their customers. We also provide those representatives who excel the opportunity to make more based on their results.

www. Vectormarketing.com

ABC Nissan

Automotive Accounting Clerk
Working as an Accounting clerk with our dealer group requires: excellent communication skills, a professional appearance, and the ability to remain calm under pressure. You must possess the confidence that comes with having a solid background in accounting, and the outgoing personality to speak up and ask questions if you need help with a project. Accounting clerks who work for our dealerships must have previous daily experience working with a computer (preferably with ADP), in a high-volume automotive accounting office, and must feel confident that they can quickly pick up on how to use our internal database. If you have the qualities described above, we would love to meet with you!

www.abcnissan.com/careers

Wells Fargo

Phone Banker

Phone Bankers are expected to sell products and services and achieve aggressive sales goals which are measured daily. Our best Phone Bankers thrive on customer interaction and never miss an opportunity to enhance the customer s relationship with Wells Fargo by marketing new products and services. They always handle each customer with a friendly, courteous touch while following strict procedures for handling various types of inquiries.

www.wellsfargo.com/careers

USAA

Unlicensed Specializes Investment Service Representative

Share our pride. Join our mission.
As a Fortune 200 financial services organization, USAA is on a mission - to facilitate the financial security of our members, the men and women of the U.S. military and their families worldwide by providing a full range of financial services and products. Headquartered on a showcase campus in San Antonio, TX, USAA attributes its long-standing success to its most valuable resource, our 26,000 employees. They are the heart and soul of our member-service culture.

www.usaa.com/careers

Cable One

Call Center Technical Care Specialist

A fantastic opportunity now exists to join Cable ONE! Serving more than 730,000 customers in 19 states with cable television, telephone, and high-speed Internet service, Cable ONE began in 1986 as a small cable television company. We are now the 10th largest cable company in the U.S., offering our residential and business consumers a wide range of the latest products and services such as HD programming, wireless Internet service, and phone service with free, unlimited long distance calling. We are looking for a motivated, driven, and energetic Technical Care Specialist Trainee to join our team in Phoenix, Arizona.

www.cableone.com

www.ingramcontent.com/pod-product-compliance
Lightning Source LLC
Chambersburg PA
CBHW050837180526
45159CB00004B/1935